The Beautiful Language of
Flowers
COLORING BOOK

John Green

Dover Publications, Inc.
Mineola, New York

A stunning array of images evokes the beauty and elegance of flowers in this unique coloring book. Thirty-one plates invite you to color these spectacular blooms, which include the amaryllis, the hibiscus, the magnolia, the peony, and the zinnia. The artist has enhanced the natural beauty of the images with a selection of outdoor creatures as well—you'll find birds, a frog, a dragonfly, butterflies, a moth, and even bees among the foliage. In addition, each illustration contains a caption identifying a symbolic meaning associated with the flower. Just select your media and experiment with the colors of your choice as you enjoy the artistic possibilities of this special collection—plus, the perforated, unbacked pages make displaying your work easy!

Copyright

Copyright © 2018 by Dover Publications, Inc.
All rights reserved.

Bibliographical Note

The Beautiful Language of Flowers Coloring Book is a new work, first published by Dover Publications, Inc., in 2018.

International Standard Book Number

ISBN-13: 978-0-486-81904-4
ISBN-10: 0-486-81904-3

Manufactured in the United States by LSC Communications
81904303   2018
www.doverpublications.com

Amaryllis ❀ *Splendid Beauty*

Anemone ❦ Sincerity

Carnation ❖ *Faithfulness*

Columbine ❧ Courage

Crocus ✤ Youthful

Daffodil ✿ *New Beginning*

Daisy ✦ *Innocence*

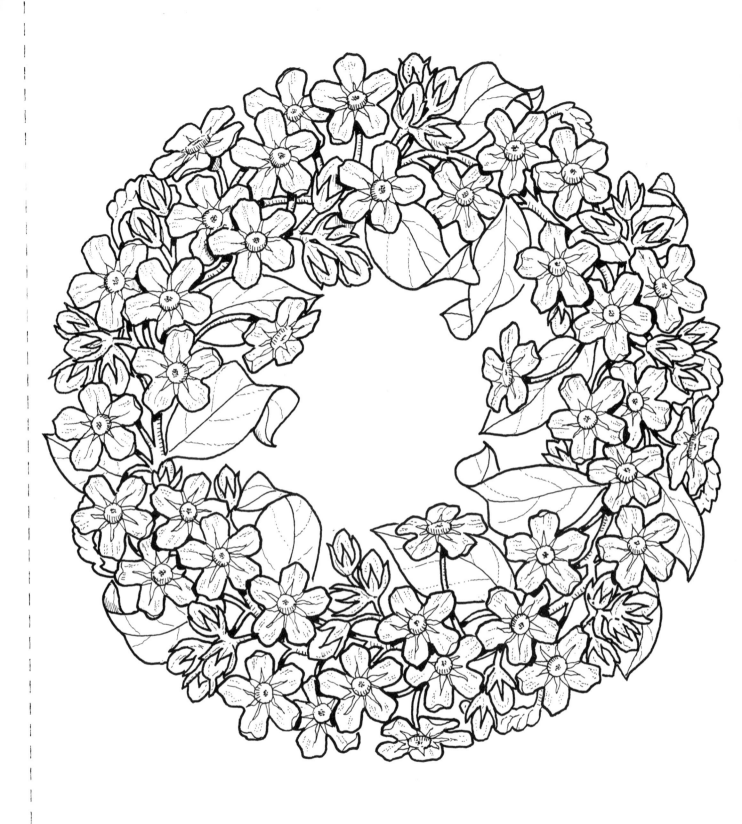

Forget-Me-Not ❧ *True Love*

Fuchsia ✤ Abundance

Hibiscus ❀ *Delicate Beauty*

Honeysuckle ✤ *Bonds of Love*

Iris ✤ Wisdom

Jasmine ✤ *Cheerfulness*

Lilac ❧ *Joy of Youth*

Lotus ❧ Truth

Magnolia ❧ *Love of Nature*

Morning Glory ❧ *Affection*

Orchid ✦ Luxury

Pansy ❦ Thoughtful Recollection

Passion Flower ✤ *Religious Devotion*

Peony �֎ Good Fortune

Poppy ❧ Extravagance

Red Rose ❧ *Love in Bloom*

Sweet Pea ❀ Bliss

Tiger Lily ❧ Friendship

Trumpet Flower ✾ *Famous*

Tulip ❀ *Declaration of Love*

Violet ✤ *Affection*

Wallflower ❋ Fidelity

Yellow Lily ✤ *Purity*